SYNOPSIS OF THE BIBLE

A Brief Survey of Its Contents and Message

(Second Edition)

Richard B. Ramsay

Synopsis of the Bible; A Brief Survey of Its Contents and Message (Second Edition)

Richard B. Ramsay

ISBN: 979-8-89860-669-5

Published by *Recursos Reformados Publishing*

Bible quotations are from the *New English Standard* version.

Contents

INTRODUCTION

The Bible is the most important book in the world, but sometimes it seems hard to understand. Many people would like to know it better, but don't know where to start. This booklet gives you a brief panoramic overview of the whole Bible so that you can find your way around more easily. It summarizes the contents, outlines the chronology, orients you with maps, and explains the main message. After reading this, you will feel more confident to study the Bible on your own.

Let's start with the most basic timeline, from beginning to end. The Bible opens with the *creation* and ends with the *new creation*. It begins with the story of Adam and Eve in the Garden of Eden and ends with the prophecy of a new earth and an eternal kingdom. In-between is the story of Jesus, the main character, our Redeemer.

Creation   Christ   New Creation
OLD TESTAMENT | NEW TESTAMENT

The plan of salvation in Christ is the main message. However, salvation is not just for individuals, but rather for the people of God as a united community. The Bible explains this plan in terms of the development of the *kingdom of God*, and all the threads of biblical history are woven together according to this theme.

The Bible is divided into two main parts, the Old Testament and the New Testament. The Old Testament covers the time before Jesus, and the New Testament includes the life of Jesus and a period of church growth several decades afterward, then concludes with prophecies of a new creation when Jesus returns. (See previous illustration.)

Biblical revelation is like a tree. A tree has roots, a trunk, and branches. In a similar way, the Bible has developed organically over a long period of time. The Old Testament forms the roots and the trunk of the Bible, while the New Testament forms the branches. The branches represent the glory of the tree, with leaves, flowers, and fruit, but the branches could not exist without the roots and the trunk.[i]

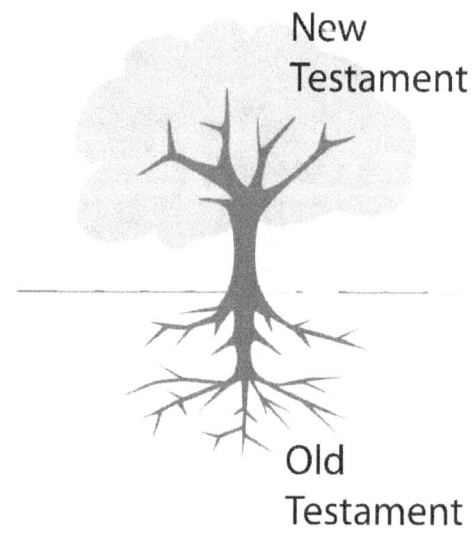

New Testament

Old Testament

Why are they called *testaments*? A testament is a legal agreement, a *covenant*. In this case, God made a covenant with His people, promising to save us through Christ. There is only one plan of salvation, and it has always been by grace through faith in Christ. People in the Old Testament looked forward to Christ, and the New Testament people saw Jesus in person, the fulfillment of all the promises.

However, there are different ways that God expressed this covenant throughout history. For example, different aspects were emphasized at the times of Adam, Noah, Abraham, Moses, and David. When Jesus came, the changes in covenant benefits were so striking that this expression was called a *new* covenant (see Hebrews 9:15). Thus Christians began dividing the Bible into the *old covenant* and the *new covenant*, or the *Old Testament* and the *New Testament*.

The Old Testament contains 39 books, and the New Testament has 27 books, totaling 66 in all.[ii] While these books were written by many different authors during a period of around 1,500 years, the Bible demonstrates incredible unity, showing that there is one divine author behind the process of composing it, as the human writers were inspired by the Holy Spirit.

> *All Scripture is breathed out by God...* (2 Timothy 3:16)

> *For no prophecy was ever produced by the will of man, but men spoke from God as they were carried along by the Holy Spirit.* (2 Peter 1:21)

THE OLD TESTAMENT

Normally the Old Testament is divided into four sections. First, we'll briefly describe each section, then we'll look at more details.

1) The Pentateuch

These first five books tell of the creation, the Fall into sin, and of the history of God's people until they enter the Promised Land, Canaan. These books lay the foundation for the plan of salvation, showing why we need to be saved and revealing the promise of the coming Savior.

2) The Historical Books

These books narrate the history of the nation of Israel from the time they enter Canaan until around four centuries before Christ. They display the hopeful development of God's people, but also show their spiritual poverty.

3) The Poetical Books

These are songs, poems, and wisdom literature of God's people during the glorious time of the monarchy, especially during the reign of David and Solomon, before God's people were divided.

4) The Prophetical Books

These are messages of repentance and hope for God's people during the difficult time of the divided kingdom.

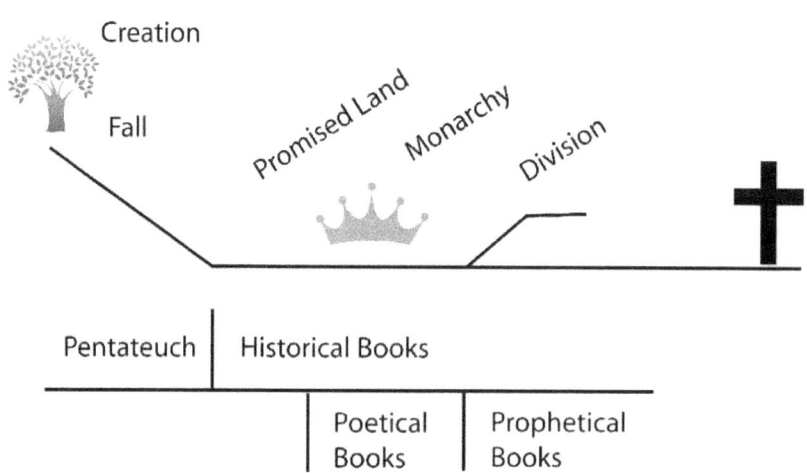

Creation

Fall

Promised Land

Monarchy

Division

Pentateuch	Historical Books		
		Poetical Books	Prophetical Books

THE PENTATEUCH

Genesis

The first book of the Bible covers more time than all the rest of the Bible together. It describes historical events of profound significance. First, God created everything in perfect harmony. He made man and woman in His own image, started the first family, gave them authority over the earth, and commanded them to take care of it.

> Then God said, "Let us make man in our image, after our likeness...." And God blessed them. And God said to them, "Be fruitful and multiply and fill the earth and subdue it...." (Genesis 1:26-28)

Man was supposed to develop a wonderful harmonious society where everyone fulfilled their purpose, loving each other and loving God. This was to be the *Kingdom of God*. However, man chose to disobey, arrogantly seeking to become independent of God. This destroyed the original harmony and derailed the development of the kingdom. After the Fall into sin (Gen. 3-4), conflict began to corrupt all relationships. There was conflict between man and God (a spiritual barrier is formed and man loses God's blessing), conflict between man and the creation (now taking care of the creation is painstaking, there are physical ailments, natural disasters, and suffering), conflict between man and other people (hatred, envy, violence, rivalry), and even conflict within man's own heart (shame, guilt, and fear).

When evil and violence became severe, God sent the Great Flood and started over with Noah and his family (Gen. 6-9). But this did not put an end to sin. When man again showed his pride and tried to become independent of God by building the Tower of Babel, God confused the world's languages and spread mankind around the globe (Gen. 11). Genesis shows the deep roots of sin and demonstrates the need for redemption.

But Genesis also shows that God's grace conquers sin and heals its terrible effects. From the very beginning we see His plan of redemption taking effect. God told Adam and Eve that their descendant would be injured in a struggle with Satan and his offspring, but that he would be victorious, striking the fatal blow (Gen. 3:15). This points to the suffering of Jesus on the cross and His victory over sin, death, and Satan.

God took away the fig leaves that Adam and Eve had used to cover themselves, which represented a pathetic attempt to cover their own guilt. Then He replaced the leaves with the skins of animals (who died to make this possible), pointing again to the sacrifice of Jesus the Lamb, who is the only one who can cover our sins (Gen. 3:7, 21, John 1:29).

As mentioned before, salvation is not just an individual matter. Salvation was always meant to restore a united body of people. Just as sin divides, salvation reunites. Thus, as Genesis continues, we see the kingdom of God taking shape in the form a growing family, then as an organized nation under God's rule.

God chose Abraham to be the father of a great multitude, called him out of Ur (in the area now called Iraq), sent him to Canaan and made a covenant with him (Gen 12-18).

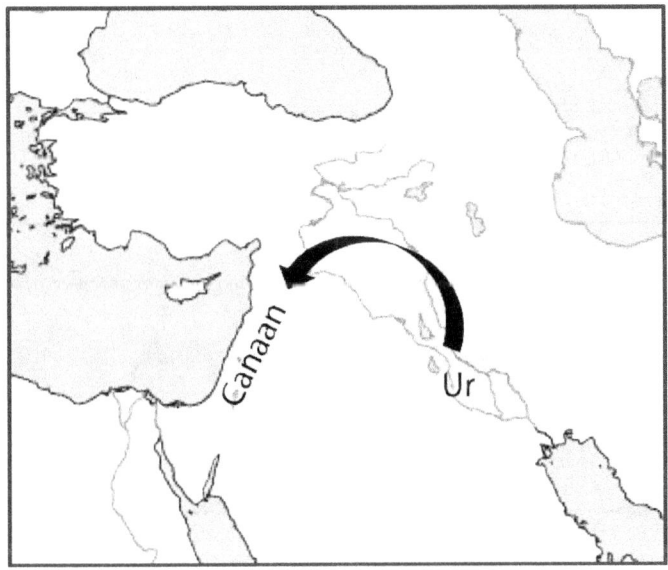

In this covenant, He demanded faithfulness and promised to bless his descendants, as well as the whole human race through them. To be specific, God promised Abraham:

a   **P**eople,
His   **P**resence, and
a   **P**lace.

The last half of Genesis shows how God's *people* began to develop as Abraham's family grew, then ended up in Egypt as slaves.

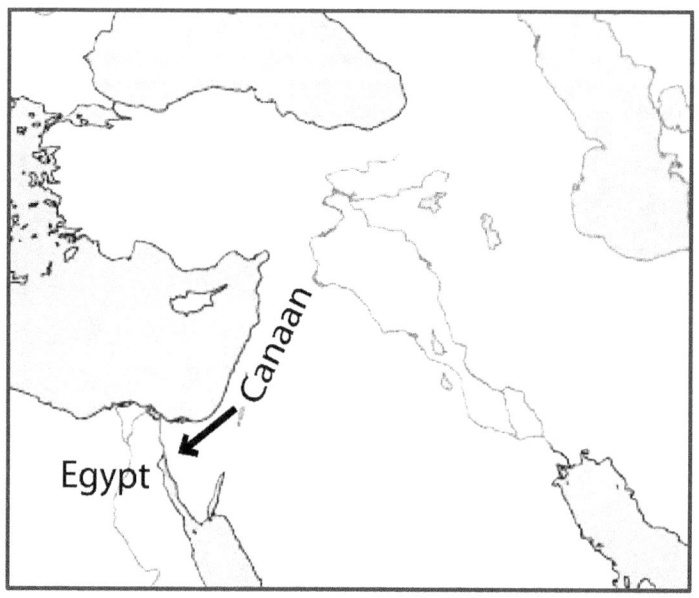

Exodus

God showed His powerful *presence* by delivering them, now a great multitude of twelve tribes, in the miraculous crossing of the Red Sea. They received the Ten Commandments at Mount Sinai, and wandered in the desert forty years, before entering Canaan, the Promised Land.

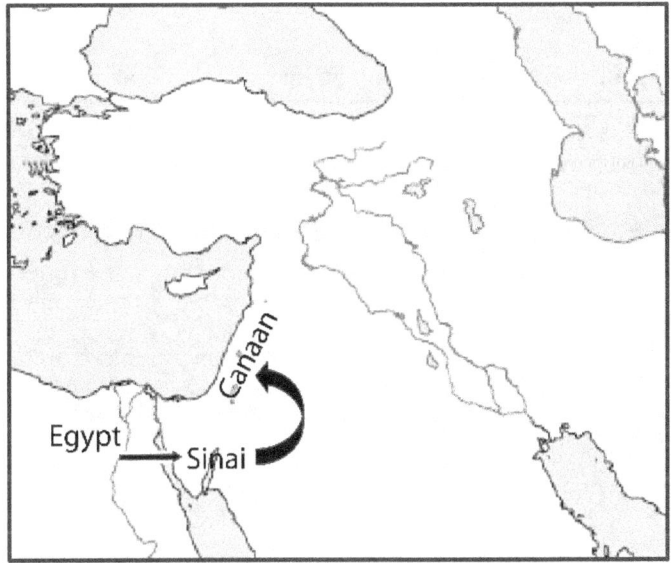

This dramatic story symbolizes salvation, our liberation from slavery to sin. It is told in *Exodus*, the second book of the Bible. Now there is a new stage of the kingdom of God, because His people are beginning to function like a *nation*, preparing to conquer the *place* God has prepared for them.

Leviticus gives regulations for the priests, called *Levites* (from the family of Levi). The tabernacle (a tent that could be moved from place to place), and later the temple (which had a similar design, but was a more permanent building in Jerusalem), were made especially to represent the *presence* of God among His people. It was to be a place of worship, a place of symbolic sacrifices, reminding them of the great sacrificial Lamb to come, and a place where God would speak to His people.

Numbers tells about a census that Israel was told to take (thus the title of the book) and about their time of wandering in the desert.

Deuteronomy also narrates some experiences in the desert and explains some of the laws given to the nation of Israel. *Deutero* means *second*, and *nomos* means *law*. Thus, *Deuteronomy* is the *repetition of the law*.

THE HISTORICAL BOOKS

The history of Israel is more exciting than any adventure movie! These Old Testament books tell of wars, murder, romance, and miracles, the conquest of Jericho, powerful Samson losing his strength because of Delilah, young David defeating the giant Goliath, older David falling for Bathsheba, and faithful Daniel surviving in the lions' den.

But the purpose is not to entertain; the history of Israel is meant to portray some of the early stages of the Kingdom of God. Israel was supposed to be an example of what God wanted all of society to be. Nevertheless, sin prevented Israel from becoming such an example; it became only a shadow of the true Kingdom of God. The very fact that Israel failed was an indication of the need for the true King.

Joshua finished the task of leading Israel into the Promised Land, and they divided the land according to the tribes of Israel. At first, God guided Israel in a direct way through the *judges*, but the people wanted a king like the other nations. The first king was Saul, followed by David and Solomon. The capital of their kingdom was Jerusalem.

In many ways, the years of these first three kings were wonderful. Israel enjoyed economic prosperity, military superiority, and cultural dominion. To a certain degree, they had received the fulfillment of the promises to Abraham: they were a new *people* in a new *place*, experiencing the *presence* of God. God renewed His covenant with David, and promised that his descendant would reign forever, pointing to the true king Jesus, who was from the family of David.

Nevertheless, moral corruption soon destroyed the kingdom, and they lost the promised blessings. Solomon had a thousand women, many of whom were foreigners and worshiped other gods. Thus, he allowed idolatry to take root in Israel, and to contaminate the religion and morality of the People of God. Then under the reign of Solomon's son Rehoboam, the nation was divided (930 B.C.), because of his oppressive policies. Samaria was the northern capital of the ten tribes (called *Israel*), while Jerusalem remained the capital of the southern two tribes (called *Judah*).

The Lord sent prophets at this time to bring them to repentance, but they continued in their sinful ways. Both Judah and Israel had one king after another, frequently characterized by violence and deceit. Finally, God used the enemy nations as His instruments to wake them up spiritually. First, Israel was taken captive by Assyria (722 B.C.), and the Israelites lost their identity as they intermingled with foreigners.

Then Judah was taken captive by Babylon, the temple in Jerusalem was destroyed (586 B.C.), and the Ark of the Covenant was lost. Years later, some returned to Jerusalem to rebuild the temple and the walls of Jerusalem, making a weak attempt to restore the kingdom of Israel. But God's *people* had practically lost their identity, they had lost their *place*, the land of Canaan, and they had lost their sense of God's *presence*.

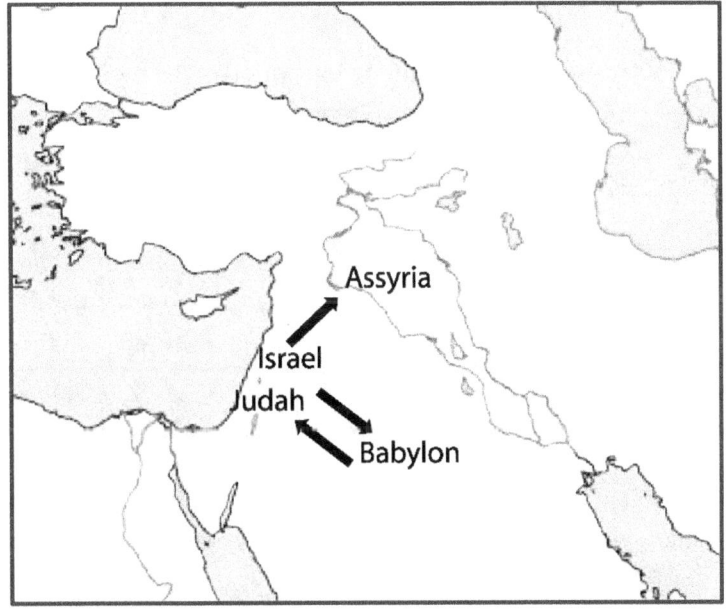

The historical books are Joshua, Judges, Ruth, 1 and 2 Samuel, 1 and 2 Kings, 1 and 2 Chronicles, Ezra, Nehemiah, and Esther.

THE POETICAL BOOKS

Biblical poetry was composed during the period of the monarchy. Most of it was written by David and Solomon. These books beautifully portray the *presence* of God among His *people*. It includes some of the most inspiring poetry of the world, such as Psalm 23.

> *The Lord is my shepherd; I shall not want. He makes me lie down in green pastures. He leads me beside still waters. He restores my soul. He leads me in paths of righteousness for his name's sake. Even though I walk through the valley of the shadow of death, I will fear no evil, for you are with me; your rod and your staff, they comfort me. (Psalm 23:1-4)*

- *Job* was the righteous man who suffered and wanted to ask God why.
- The *Psalms* are the songbook of the Bible.
- *Proverbs* are jewels of wisdom.
- *Ecclesiastes* tells of a spiritual pilgrimage, a man seeking true meaning in life.
- *Song of Songs* is a beautiful love song, reflecting God's love for His people.
- *Lamentations* laments the destruction of Jerusalem.

THE PROPHETICAL BOOKS

During the time of the divided kingdom, God spoke to His people through prophetical preachers, calling them to repentance, offering forgiveness, and telling of the coming Messiah. (The term *Messiah* is translated as *Christ* in Greek and literally means *the anointed one*. It refers to someone designated for a special task.) Their messages are recorded in the prophetical books. In these sections of the Bible, we see that God had not totally removed His presence, and that in spite of the Israelites' unfaithfulness, God would still keep His promises. It is here that God's grace becomes astonishing. There is no doubt that God's people *do not deserve* His blessings, but in spite of that, God will show His infinite love and forgiveness. As we read these books, we can identify with Israel, and we rejoice in God's limitless mercy.

The prophets are normally divided into the "major" prophets and the "minor" prophets, according to their length. (Lamentations is placed after Jeremiah in the Bible, since he is considered to be the author of both, so sometimes it is included as one of the prophetical books. But the style and contents of Lamentations are more poetical than prophetical.)

The "major" prophets are, in their order in the Bible: Isaiah, Jeremiah, Ezekiel, and Daniel. The "minor" prophets are, in order: Hosea, Joel, Amos, Obadiah, Jonah, Micah, Nahum, Habakkuk, Zephaniah, Haggai, Zechariah, and Malachi. An easy way to remember these minor prophets in their proper order is to memorize two rhythmic phrases using the first two or three letters of the names, as follows: "Ho-Jo-Am-Ob-Jo, Mi-Na-Hab-Ze-Hag-Ze-Ma." It may sound funny at first, but once you learn this phrase, you will be surprised how it helps!

The Old Testament revelation ends around four hundred years before the time of Christ's birth. Israel waits for God to break His silence, and they wait for the Messiah. During these four centuries, the Jewish people are ruled by several different nations. Under Alexander the Great, the whole region of the Middle East comes under the influence of the Greek language and culture. This influence continued through the time of the New Testament, even when the Romans were ruling. While the Old Testament had been written in Hebrew (except for brief portions in Aramaic), the New Testament would be written in Greek.

DATES OF THE OLD TESTAMENT

The easiest years to remember are for Abraham and David. Abraham lived around 2,000 B.C., and David lived around 1,000 B.C. The exact date of the exodus is debated among scholars, but the other dates below are widely accepted.

KEY OLD TESTAMENT DATES

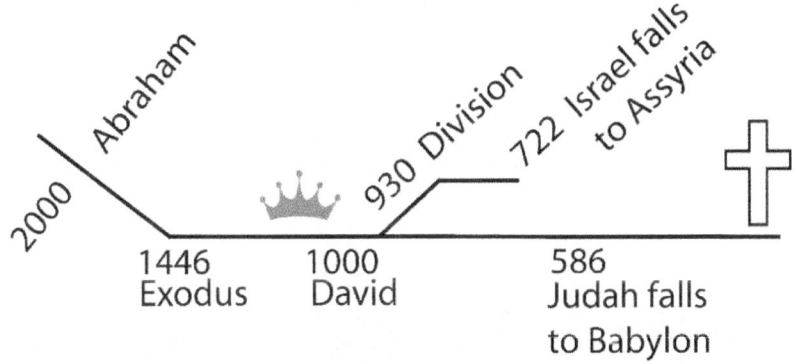

THE NEW TESTAMENT

The Old Testament makes it clear that the Kingdom of God cannot be established without first resolving the problem of sin and its effects. Man needs to be reconciled with God and liberated from the dominion of sin before he can develop a society that lives according to God's principles.

For this reason, Jesus came to live a perfect life, die on the cross for our sins, and conquer death in His resurrection. Jesus saves us from sin and its consequences, restoring our relationship with God, with others, with ourselves, and eventually even with the broken creation. Each person who puts his faith in Him personally begins to participate in the new kingdom. This plan of salvation is the central message of the Bible.

The New Testament can be divided into four sections:

1) The Gospels
They tell the amazing story of Jesus.

2) Acts
This book relates the incredible expansion of the Kingdom.

3) The Epistles
These letters give practical and theological pastoral teaching for the churches.

4) Revelation
This unusual book is a prophecy of the final victory in Christ, a vision of heaven opened.

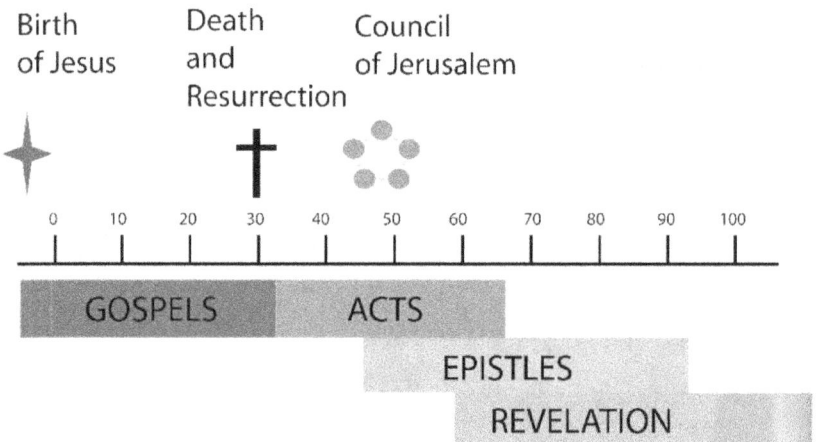

THE GOSPELS

The gospels proclaim that the true kingdom of God has come, because the true King is here. What the people of the Old Testament could not do, Jesus does. Jesus is the fresh new branch miraculously growing out of the dead tree trunk of Israel (Isaiah 11:1).

Jesus was born in Bethlehem, was taken to Egypt as a baby because king Herod wanted to kill Him (Mt. 2:13), then returned to Nazareth where He grew up. He spent most of His three years of public ministry around the Sea of Galilee. His last days on earth were spent in Jerusalem, where He was finally crucified and rose from the dead. Forty days later He ascended into heaven as the disciples watched Him.

Jesus shows by His miracles and His teaching that He is God Himself *present* among us. Jesus gathers His disciples and begins to form a new *people*, not of the Jewish nation, but now of believers in all nations and from all ethnic groups (Matthew 28:18-20). He says that He will go away, but He promises that He will return to make a new *place* for us, a new heaven and a new earth. At the last supper, Jesus breaks the bread and serves the wine to the disciples saying,

> *This is my blood of the covenant, which is poured out for many for the forgiveness of sins. I tell you I will not drink again of this fruit of the vine until that day when I drink it new with you in my Father's kingdom. (Matthew 26:28-29)*

Salvation did not come without a great cost. Since God is just, he had to punish sin. These were the terms of the covenant. However, since God is also merciful, He wanted to save His people. Therefore, He punished sin in the person of His own Son, instead of us. This manifests

His astonishing love and grace. The wrath of God that we all deserved fell upon Jesus. He became like a "black hole" that sucks all evil into His own soul, then He destroys it.

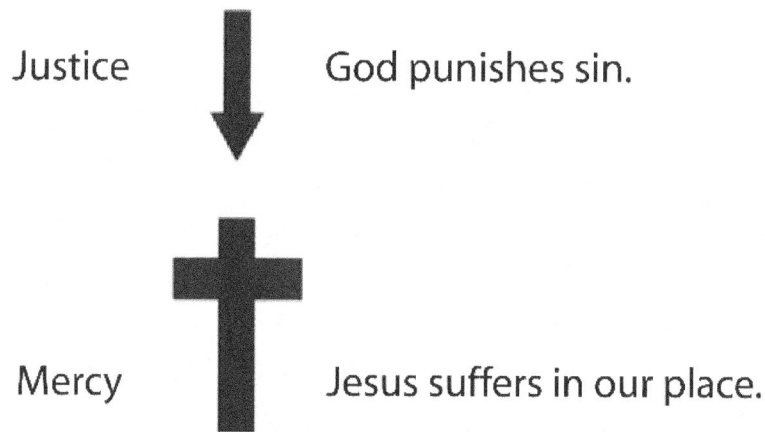

Justice   God punishes sin.

Mercy   Jesus suffers in our place.

This is why Jesus cried out from the cross, "My God, my God, why have you forsaken me?" (Matthew 27:46). Because He was voluntarily taking our sin upon Himself, in that moment He was actually suffering separation from the Father.

Why are there four gospels? Because each one presents a distinct, but not contradictory, perspective:

Matthew wrote especially to Jewish readers to show that Jesus was the Messiah, fulfilling Old Testament prophecy.

Mark wrote probably to Gentile (non-Jewish) believers in Rome, making the history a little simpler, emphasizing the events in Jesus' life more than His teachings.

Luke wrote to a man named Theophilus, telling a more ordered life of Christ (Luke 1:1-4). His gospel is longer and more detailed.

John wrote a more theological gospel, simple but profound, with the express purpose that the readers might "believe that Jesus is the Christ, the Son of God, and that by believing you may have life in his name." (John 20:31). The readers were not from any particular group, but from the whole world, including Jews and Gentiles.

ACTS

The Book of Acts relates the preaching of the gospel to the "ends of the earth" and the growth of the Church. God's *presence* is now manifested especially in the person of the Holy Spirit.

> *But you will receive power when the Holy Spirit has come upon you, and you will be my witnesses in Jerusalem and in all Judea and Samaria, and to the end of the earth.* (Acts 1:8)

The great expansion begins in Jerusalem on the day of Pentecost, when the Holy Spirit is poured out on the apostles. Peter preaches a very special sermon in Jerusalem, and thousands are converted. After this, the gospel spreads to the regions of Judea and Samaria, and finally Paul and others travel from Antioch throughout the whole Mediterranean area, including Asia Minor, Greece, and Rome, where Paul is imprisoned.

The Book of Acts shows that Jesus has won the victory, and that He has sent the Spirit to continue the work of redemption. The book clearly highlights the fact that not only Jews believe, but also the Gentiles (term used for the non-Jews). While there were some Gentile believers in the Old Testament, now the main growth of the Church is among them. The *people* of God are now believers from all nations and all ethnic groups.

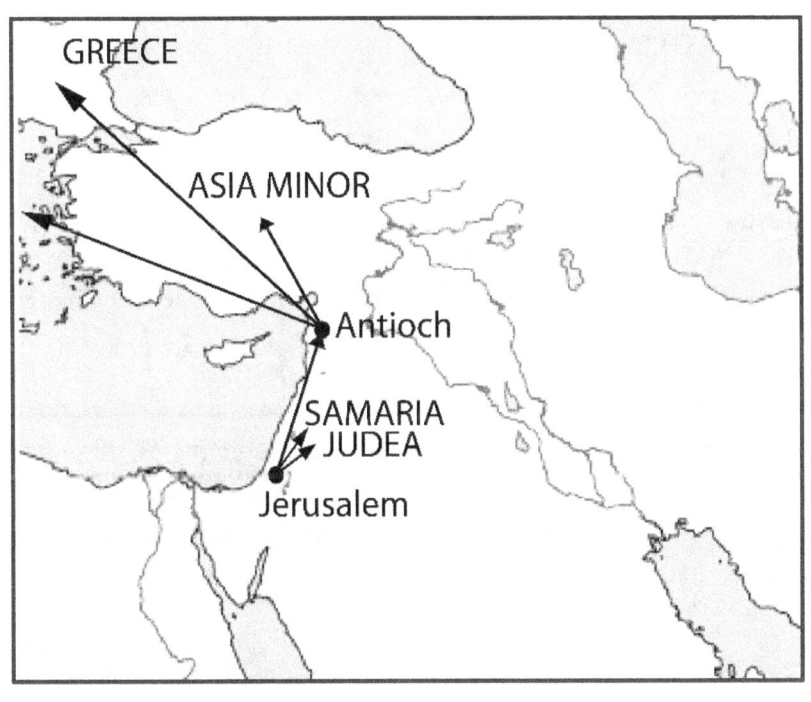

GREECE

ASIA MINOR

Antioch

SAMARIA
JUDEA

Jerusalem

THE EPISTLES

Paul wrote most of the New Testament letters. His purpose was to encourage new believers in their spiritual growth and explain the meaning of salvation in Christ. *Romans* is the most theological of the letters. It explains that we are saved by faith. All people are sinners, deserving eternal condemnation, but by trusting Christ and what He accomplished in His death and resurrection, we can be forgiven and receive eternal life.

Paul's other letters are the following: *1 and 2 Corinthians, Galatians, Ephesians, Philippians, Colossians, 1 and 2 Thessalonians, 1 and 2 Timothy, Titus,* and *Philemon.* In his letters, Paul often speaks of salvation in terms of becoming part of the kingdom of God.

> *He has delivered us from the domain of darkness and transferred us to the kingdom of his beloved Son, in whom we have redemption, the forgiveness of sins.* (Colossians 1:13-14)

Hebrews is written to show that Christ is superior to the angels and any human priest. The author is anonymous. The other letters that are not by Paul have the names of their authors: *James, 1 and 2 Peter, 1, 2 y 3 John*, and *Jude.*

REVELATION

Revelation is one of the most glorious books of the Bible. It contains colorful images and dramatic scenes, symbolizing important events, nations, and divine beings. It opens the windows of heaven to show us scenes of Christ in His glory, with celestial beings that worship God day and night. The purpose is to encourage Christians in the midst of suffering, since at the time it was written, they were being persecuted. It contains prophecies about the second coming of Christ, but the purpose is not to give us a detailed chronology of the end of this world. It reveals a general perspective of the victory of Christ over Satan, ending with a scene of the New Jerusalem. Contrary to a common misunderstanding, the Bible does *not* teach that we will become winged angels flying around in heaven, but rather that we will live eternally in the presence of the Lord on a new earth, in renovated resurrected bodies.

> *They shall hunger no more, neither thirst anymore; the sun shall not strike them, nor any scorching heat. For the Lamb in the midst of the throne will be their shepherd, and he will guide them to springs of living water, and God will wipe away every tear from their eyes.* (Revelation 7:16-17)

> *Then I saw a new heaven and a new earth, for the first heaven and the first earth had passed away, and the sea was no more. And I saw the holy city, new Jerusalem, coming down out of heaven from God....* (Revelation 21:1-2)

> *And behold, I am coming soon.* (Revelation 22:7)

The kingdom of God will be finally established in its complete and eternal form. The victory will be won, and salvation will be finished. His *people* will be believers from every tribe, tongue, people and nation. We will see Him *face to face* and live in His glorious and loving *presence* for eternity. And we will have an eternal *place*, a new earth and a new heaven, totally restored with no effects of sin or corruption. There is no need for the sun or moon because the glory of God gives sufficient light (Revelation 21). We don't know all the details of the new heaven and the new earth, but we do know that it will be absolutely perfect and that we will be totally satisfied and filled with joy, because we will be in His presence. Hallelujah!

The following table summarizes the different stages of the Kingdom of God, with the fulfillments and losses of the promises.

SUMMARY OF THE PROMISES OF THE KINGDOM OF GOD

PROMISE	Fulfillment in the O.T.	Loss of the Promise in the O.T.	Fulfillment in the N.T.	Fulfillment when Jesus returns
1. PEOPLE	The Nation of Israel	Division and Captivity	All Believers	All Believers Glorified
2. PRESENCE	The Temple	The Temple Destroyed	Jesus and the Holy Spirit	We See Him Face to Face in His Glory.
3. PLACE	Canaan	Canaan Under Foreign Dominion	The Whole Earth	New Heavens and New Earth

DATES OF THE NEW TESTAMENT

Observe the following key dates for the New Testament history.

1) The birth of Jesus: around 4-6 B.C.

The date for the birth of Jesus may surprise you. This does not indicate any errors in the biblical accounts. It only shows that when historians started dividing history between B.C. and A.D., they didn't have all the proper information. Historians now know that Herod died in 4 B.C. According to the biblical account, Herod tried to kill Jesus when He was a small baby (Matthew 2:13-16). Therefore, Jesus would have been born not long before that date.

2) The death and resurrection of Jesus: 30 or 33 A.D.

Luke 3:23 says that Jesus was "about 30 years old" when He began His public ministry. This could be several years older than 30. His ministry lasted around three years, according to the number of Passovers suggested in the Gospel of John. Scholars try to coordinate statements in the gospels with the Jewish calendar, and suggest that his crucifixion was probably either in 30 A.D. or in 33 A.D.

3) The Council of Jerusalem: 48 A.D.

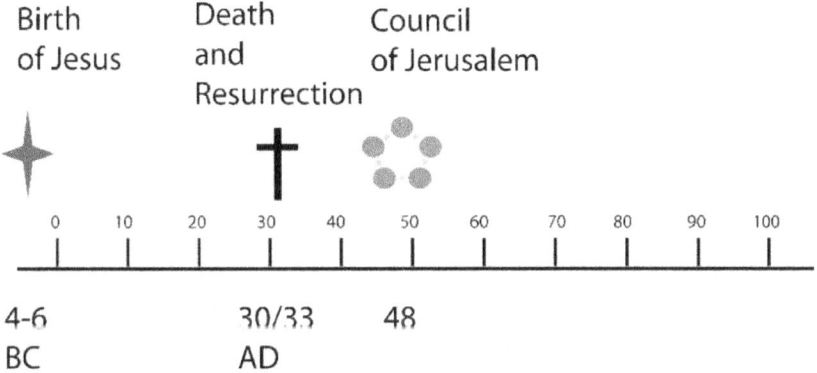

Birth of Jesus
Death and Resurrection
Council of Jerusalem

0   10   20   30   40   50   60   70   80   90   100

4-6 BC   30/33 AD   48

Brief Summary of the Contents of the Books of the Bible

Old Testament

PENTATEUCH	
Genesis	The beginnings of creation, man, sin, and salvation
Exodus	Liberation from slavery in Egypt
Leviticus	Regulations for the Levites
Numbers	The census and wandering in the desert
Deuteronomy	Repetition of the law

HISTORICAL BOOKS	
Joshua	Entering the Promised Land
Judges	War with neighboring nations
Ruth	Moabite woman who became part of Israel
1 and 2 Samuel	Lives of Samuel, Saul, and David
1 and 2 Kings	Solomon and other kings until the captivity
1 and 2 Chronicles	Another account of Israel from Saul to the captivity
Ezra	Rebuilding the temple in Jerusalem after captivity
Nehemiah	Rebuilding the walls of Jerusalem after captivity
Esther	Jewish woman made queen of Persia during captivity

POETICAL BOOKS	
Job	A righteous man suffers and wants to ask God why.
Psalms	The songbook of Israel
Proverbs	Jewels of wisdom
Ecclesiastes	A spiritual pilgrimage, seeking the meaning of life
Song of Songs	A love song that reflects God's love for His people
Lamentations	Laments the destruction of Jerusalem.

THE MAJOR PROPHETS	
Isaiah	Calls Judah to repentance because of their injustice. Comforts them with the news of future restoration and the coming Messiah.
Jeremiah	Judah must repent of their unfaithfulness.
Ezekiel	Visions of God's judgment and the future restoration of Jerusalem
Daniel	This prophet confronts Nebuchadnezzar, king of Babylon.

THE MINOR PROPHETS	
Hosea	God loves even His unfaithful people.
Joel	The Day of the Lord, devastating judgment
Amos	Denounces Israel for living in luxury at the expense of the poor.
Obadiah	The neighbor nation, Edom, will be punished for invading Judah.
Jonah	The prophet flees, is swallowed by a great fish, is rescued by God, and finally takes God's message to Nineveh.
Micah	Reproach for exploitation of the poor and for perversion of the priesthood
Nahum	Prophesies destruction of Nineveh.
Habakkuk	The prophet doubts God's justice.
Zephaniah	Judgment on Judah and other nations
Haggai	Encourages the returnees to reconstruct the temple.
Zechariah	Visions of restoration and of the Messiah
Malachi	Accusations of God against the priests

New Testament

THE GOSPELS AND ACTS	
Matthew	He wrote especially to Jewish readers to show that Jesus was the Messiah, fulfilling Old Testament prophecy.
Mark	He wrote probably to Gentile (non-Jewish) believers in Rome, making the history a little more simple, emphasizing the events in Jesus' life more than His teachings.
Luke	He wrote to a man named Theophilus, telling a more ordered life of Christ. (Luke 1:1-4). His gospel is longer and detailed.
John	He wrote a more theological gospel, with the express purpose that the readers might "believe that Jesus is the Christ, the Son of God, and that believing, they might have life in His name" (John 20:31). The readers were not from any particular group, but from the whole world, Jews and Gentiles.
Acts	The preaching of the gospel and the expansion of the kingdom in the power of the Holy Spirit

THE EPISTLES AND REVELATION	
Romans	We are saved by grace through faith.
1 Corinthians	Corrects problems of division and immorality.
2 Corinthians	Paul defends his own ministry.
Galatians	Corrects legalism.
Ephesians	Unity in Christ
Philippians	Joy in the midst of suffering
Colossians	New life in Christ
1 and 2 Thessalonians	The second coming of Christ.
1 and 2 Timothy	Counsel for a young pastor.
Titus	Instructions for leaders in Crete.
Philemon	Paul asks Philemon to receive Onesimus, his ex-slave, as a brother.
Hebrews	The superiority of Christ
James	Corrects false view of moral freedom.
1 and 2 Peter	Encourages them to have hope.
1, 2, and 3 John	God is light and love.
Jude	We should resist false teachers.
Revelation	We will have victory in Christ and the kingdom will be established in its complete and eternal form.

REVIEW QUESTIONS

Introduction

1. The Bible begins with the narration of the _____ and ends with the prophecy of _____.
2. Who is the main character of the Bible?
3. What is the main message of the Bible?
4. All of the threads of Bible history can be woven together according to what theme?
5. The Bible explains God's relationship with His people in terms of a _____.
6. What is the meaning of this way in which God relates with His people? What practical importance does it have for us?

The Old Testament

1. Why are the two main parts of the Bible called the Old Testament and the New Testament?
2. How many books are there in the Bible (Protestant version)?
3. How many years did the process take to compose the whole Bible?
4. Quote a Bible passage that teaches that the Bible is inspired by God.
5. If the Bible is like a tree, what part represents the Old Testament, and what part represents the New Testament?
6. Name the four sections of the Old Testament and give a brief description of their contents.

The Pentateuch

1. God created everything in perfect _____.
2. God made man and women in His _____.
3. God commanded man to _____ the earth.

4. Explain the effects of sin.
5. Why did God send the Great Flood?
6. What did God do when man built the Tower of Babel?
7. In what two ways do we see signs of the plan of redemption in the Garden of Eden?
8. What three promises did God make to Abraham?
9. How did God begin to form His people through Abraham?
10. Where did the family of Abraham become enslaved?
11. How did they get out of that slavery?
12. What did God's people receive on Mount Sinai?
13. What does the history in the book of *Exodus* symbolize?
14. After receiving the law, the people of God began to function as a _____.
15. Describe the contents of *Leviticus*.
16. What was the tabernacle?
17. Describe the contents of *Numbers*.
18. Describe the contents of *Deuteronomy*.

The Historical Books

1. Israel was supposed to be an _____ of what God wanted for all of _____.
2. Who finished the task of taking Israel into the Promised Land?
3. Name the three kings of Israel during the "glorious" years.
4. How did Solomon permit religious corruption in Israel?
5. Explain why Israel was divided. In what year was it divided?
6. What names were given to each part of God's people after the division?
7. Name the capital city of each part of God's people during the division.
8. Give the key information regarding the conquest of Israel.
9. Give the key information regarding the conquest of Judah.
10. Describe the return from captivity to Jerusalem. What tasks did they complete?

The Poetical Books

1. Who wrote most of the poetry of the Old Testament?

2. In what period was it written?
3. Briefly describe the content of Job, Psalms, Proverbs, Ecclesiastes, Song of Songs, and Lamentations.

The Prophetic Books

1. Give a brief summary of the general message of the prophets.
2. What does *Messiah* mean?
3. When did the writings of the Old Testament end?
4. What was the political situation of Israel during the four centuries before Christ?
5. What culture influenced the Middle East region during the period shortly before Christ?
6. In what language was the Old Testament written? The New Testament?

Dates of the Old Testament

Write the corresponding year beside each key person or event of the Old Testament:

      Abraham
      The exodus
      David
      The division
      Assyria conquers Israel.
      Babylon conquers Judah.

The New Testament

1. Why did Jesus come?
2. Name the four sections of the New Testament and briefly describe the content of each.

The Gospels

1. Where was Jesus born? Where did he grow up? Where did he spend most of the time of his adult ministry? Where did he die?
2. How did God manifest both His justice and His mercy in the death of Christ?
3. Briefly describe the differences between the four gospels.

Acts

1. What is the main theme of Acts?
2. In the Book of Acts, the presence of God is manifested especially in the person of _____.
3. The Book of Acts clearly highlights the fact that not only the Jews believe, but also the _____.

The Epistles

1. Who wrote the majority of the epistles of the New Testament?
2. What is the purpose of the letters?
3. Briefly describe the contents of *Romans*.
4. Paul speaks of salvation in terms of becoming part of _____.

Revelation

1. What is the purpose of *Revelation*?
2. Briefly summarize the contents of the book of Revelation.
3. Describe some of the characteristics of the complete and eternal form of the kingdom of God.

Summary of the Promises of the Kingdom of God

Fill in the spaces of the table of the promises of the kingdom.

Promise	Fulfillment in the O.T.	Loss of the Promise in the O.T.	Fulfillment in the N.T.	Fulfillment when Jesus returns
1.				
2.				
3.				

Dates of the New Testament

Write the corresponding dates for each important event of the New Testament:

      The birth of Jesus
      The death and resurrection of Jesus
      The Council of Jerusalem

The Author

Dr. Ramsay was a missionary in Chile for 21 years, teaching in a seminary and planting churches. There he met his wife, Angelica. They now live in Florida and they have two adult children. For the past 25 years, they have worked internationally in distance education, traveling to teach classes and producing resources for theological education and leadership training. Richard has taught for *Universidad FLET* and *Thirdmill Seminary* and has developed many online courses.

He holds a D.Min. degree and an M.Div. from *Westminster Theological Seminary*, as well as a Th.M. from *Covenant Theological Seminary.*

Other books by the author include *The Certainty of Faith, Am I Good Enough?, Basic Greek and Exegesis, Intellectual Integrity, Transformed into the Image of Jesus, Strengthen Your Faith, Catholics and Protestants, Putting the Pieces Together,* and *Orientation for Leaders.*

NOTES

---

[i]This illustration is based on the idea of Geerhardus Vos in *Biblical Theology: Old and New Testaments*. Grand Rapids, MI: Eerdmans, 1948.

[ii]The Roman Catholic Church also includes a few other "apocryphal" books. The rest are the same as in the Protestant Bible. For the purposes of this booklet, the reader may use a Catholic Bible if he wishes.

www.ingramcontent.com/pod-product-compliance
Lightning Source LLC
Chambersburg PA
CBHW071220130626
46555CB00004B/1781